GET REAL,

GET RID,

AND GET GOING ®

A short study and introduction to
FEARLESS GROWTH®

Becky Michel

GET REAL, GET RID, AND GET GOING®

A short study and introduction to FEARLESS GROWTH®

Creative Expressions Publishing

Cover design by Becky Michel

Printed in the United States of America

ISBN # 979-8-88680-136-1
GET REAL, GET RID, AND GET GOING – A introduction into the three-part Fearless Growth book series.
Fearless growth starts with getting real, moves into being able to surrender to the setbacks and becoming consciously aware enough to grow with intent. Intentional change is necessary to experience real true Fearless Growth.

Fearless Growth™ Leader and Expert
Becky Michel

About Becky

 **Fearless Growth Expert** – Becky Michel is the Author & Creator of Fearless Growth®. She has applied and shared this process for over a decade.

Author – of the three-part Fearless Growth® series as well as a series of children's self-help books. All publications are from a faith-based perspective. Fearless Growth® is a lifelong process. It is a journey to become exactly who God created you to be. God gave Becky Fearless Growth® to begin changing herself and then to help others. Change, choice, and challenge abound at the core of living a Fearless Growth® life. You must want to change your beliefs, actions, and mindset.

Speaker – Becky brings an inspiring message of becoming the person God created you to be by standing up for yourself throughout that renovation process–Fearless Growth®. She shows you how to live life on purpose and push through the challenges that hold you back from experiencing growth and freedom in Christ so you can live free from addictions, childhood grievances, and the daily struggles of life.

Coach – Becky offers a Fearless Growth® coaching program that is "Real Life" constructed. It is about being honest with yourself about who and where you are. You will begin the process of change today, yet you will not do it alone! Let Becky help you discover–Fearless Growth®!

Creative Expressions is a division of Becky Michel.

For booking or more information, contact Becky at:

BeckyMichel.com

417-293-5340

Becky@BeckyMichel.com

Table of Contents

Introduction

Growth is a repetitious process. A journey of failing forward many times throughout life. If you want to dig deeper into Fearless Growth®, the meaning and Biblical truths behind it, you will want to order the three-book series of Fearless Growth®, No Shame, No Fear, and No Limits. If you want to gain deeper understanding and instruction pertaining to fear, growth, realness, love, and becoming who God wants you to, along with hearing more of a Fearless Growth® personal story, you'll find that in the books. This is a short study introduction I created to give you a sample of digging deeper and help you assess if Fearless Growth® is something you desire to experience in your own life. Fearless Growth® is something God has given me the ability to not only put together over the past ten years, but live it each day. Experience real lasting change through Fearless Growth®, a three-part short read book series.

If you are interested in having Becky, come speak at your next event, conference, or meeting, please use the contact info in this book or via her website. Visit BeckyMichel.Com to order books.

get real

GROWTH IS A CHOICE

There's nothing in the world like having a vision, a calling, a work to do, knowing deep down in the core of your soul that this is something you were put here for. Your divine purpose. Yet you are completely lacking direction in knowing how to start, where to go, and the details of this calling. Which way do you turn, how do you get there? Doesn't make a bit of sense does it? How can you be so certain yet so uncertain about the same thing simultaneously? That's exactly how I have felt about a calling, ever since God put it in me several years ago! All I knew is that in addition to the best and greatest callings of being a wife and mom I was to help people, God said I want you to share your story. Little did I know that day was going to be a ten plus year journey before I would actually be able to do this work in the capacity of which God called me to. In fact, around year seven was the first time I began to get some clarity, then the years to follow were even more so as finally, that puzzle started coming together. Have you ever felt a little spark, or a constant burning flame, it was something you had to do? Something that will etch on your heart forever if you are unable to fulfill it, even if it's something as simple as going to another person to make things right in the relationship, or having an important conversation with someone. If that's you, you're in good company.

God's word says...

When we feel overwhelmed because of our sins or the poor choices and bad habits we choose, those are the times God is waiting to hear from us. We need to repent and renew our fellowship with Him. Not only do the consequences of what we do hurt ourselves but others around us as well. Self-discipline is not easy. Being disciplined by God is the worse discipline I've ever received. It's painful, uncomfortable, and can really cause you to sweat it, no pun intended. I've personally been on that hot seat many times, and it's a hard seat to sit on and it's also a choice, as God gives us free will to either obey or disobey. When we are at our weakest, God's power takes on added significance for us. The Lord will be a refuge for the oppressed, a refuge in times of trouble. Read Psalm 61-63.

Maybe you have wanted to start a business, write a book, travel somewhere, or simply be a part of something bigger than yourself? These dreams are there for a reason, to fulfill our purpose, to encourage our faith, and to strengthen us as humans. Giving us hope and growing us fearlessly, when we learn the art of surrender. See my friend; I didn't know the art of surrendering for quite some time after God put a message and mission in me. With surrender comes great faith, patience, hope, courage, and the ability to be still and know God. All things I thought I knew, but as it turned out, I'm still learning, to this day, matter of fact. I believe we never stop growing, or at least we shouldn't if we love God and want to be filled with more of Him.

God's word says...

There are so many examples of faith, hope, courage, and growth in God's word, which makes it hard to choose the right scripture to expand upon. I personally like the lessons of the parables. The story of the wheat and the tares in the book of Matthew shows the example of two types of people. Those who want God's will in their lives and are willing to submit to Him and take the discipline, and choose growth then those who maybe don't even realize it, but have chosen to go in the opposite direction, which means they have submitted to the control of Satan. This scripture shows us that if we do not choose God, we choose Satan by default. Have you ever been in a situation where you knew what you needed to do but still chose the thing that was most appealing to your flesh? I would say it is safe to say we all have done this at sometime in our lives, but the important thing is that we learn to become self-aware, by examining ourselves, and learn to correct the poor choices or the times we choose Satan by default. This doesn't mean we are bad people it just means we have some work to do. Trust me, I've been there so many times in my life.

Sometimes the hardest things are the simplest things, yet take so long to learn. Why don't we get it, why can't we just see it? Because it's part of the journey! Life is a process, and when we are able to see the process for what it is, it is truly priceless! The things we learn, the places God puts us, the relationships we develop along the journey, and the growth we experience…it's priceless. The ill-fated part of this is that we have to move along on down that race of life and up that ladder of growth in order to be able to look back over the past five, or ten, or twenty years and say "I see it now", "oh, I get it". My life has been a process, I have been on a journey.

The important thing to remember is not to get cooked in the squat, as Zig Ziglar would say. Getting cooked in the squat is a process of putting off the things we are certain we need to do and ignoring what we know we shouldn't, and before you know it, life has gotten away and time has passed by. Maybe it's rejecting God's gentle tug when He's pushing or pulling on you, working a certain job or volunteering somewhere you know you probably should have done or participated in. Maybe it's not so much the things we didn't quite get around to, but the things that we flat out left undone or walked away from because we just didn't want to take the time, or make the effort. Sure, that's a hard pill to swallow, but the best thing you can do right now, is simply pray and start no matter where you are or are not. Starting over is a great place to be.

The first part of Fearless Growth is getting real. In order to do this, honesty, humility, and heart must come into play. So many people are unwilling to do the hard things in order to move forward and grow. Spiritual and personal growth is actually super hard when it's intentional. It involves a constant examination and a consistent dying to self, it's ugly, it's messy, and can often be humiliating. But oh, the places you will go once you choose to do it. Surrendering to your struggles is the first and most important step in Fearless Growth®. Can you do it alone? This is something to be learn through Fearless Growth. Imagine a bar about eye level, you can apply the Fearless

Growth® process and tools and no matter what, it will definitely help you. However, without God you will only be able to get to that bar, versus if you would have had His guidance and grace. Now you can go sky high because it takes it off of you, and no longer are you doing it in your own self, but rather, in Him. These touchy subjects are very hard to deal with, sometimes very emotionally exhausting. When you have a personal relationship with Christ you can rest in freely giving it all to Him. He is the great comforter. So yes, you can do it in yourself but you can't get the full measure of peace that passes all understanding without God. Within Him is where we can take those attributes of faith, hope, patience, courage, and being still to a much greater level. Don't get to the end of your race and look around to realize because you we're unwilling to do the hard things, to empty the baggage, and to get real, you not only hurt yourself, but it affected others as well, and now it's too late to do some of the crap God had placed in front of you. Again, it's never to late to repent, change, start over, and grow, but missed opportunities are just that, missed.

God's word says...

For him to know to do good and do it not, to him it is sin. Which pretty much sums up what I just wrote. Oh, how many times I have sinned, and continue to do so. Sometimes without though, and sometimes not using my head, and sometimes willfully. My personal goal is for the willful sins to become les and les as I grow. I remember a time I lived in bondage to my band aids and bad behaviors. I use to believe that God was disappointed in me, and I mostly seen the bad in me and the wrong I would do. When I discovered God's unconditional love for me and the fact, He has already defeated the enemy and won victory over the struggles I personally have had and have, I began to see myself in a more positive light, and I began to realize I had gifts and strengths and was highly favored by my father. So, while we have a sinful nature, we should also remember that we were created in the likeness of God. There is excellence and dignity inherent in being human that we should greatly consider as we understand our greater potential. Which by the way, goes both ways, potential for good as well as bad, and that is the free will we each are given.

I love to sing, but the reality of that fact is that I suck at it. I really do. I was not born with the natural ability to carry a tune. Does that mean I should stop singing? Or that I can't learn to improve? No, scripture tells us to make a joyful noise doesn't it? I do however believe that there are times we must come to the hard realizations of very personal matters. Those difficult times when you do some self-examining and learn to be brutally honest with yourself. You realize you just can't do it on your own or in the way you had planned. Maybe that's a business, or a relationship, or an addiction. Maybe you push people away, are too bossy, too argumentative, or you struggle to be friendly therefore lack true friends. Perhaps you don't know much, but you always act as though you do. Who likes a no it all? Who knows a know it all? Who is a know it all? Or maybe you are like me and have a ton of things I can't do that others excel at. Have you ever had to swallow your pride with apology after standing your ground about something or standing up to someone only to realize how wrong you had been? I have! Dang those are hard times. Those are the times we have to fall on our faces, cry out and often times ask for help. If I don't know something, or can't seem to stop something, it doesn't mean I'm not smart or I am not good at anything, it just means I don't about know that particular thing. It means I need someone who has gone before me to show me the way. If you have lived long at all, you have needed help. We all have times we get down in those valleys of life and can use a hand, and there's no shame in that. Not only does it allow us to practice humility, but it also gives someone else the opportunity to be a blessing, and if you have ever helped someone out of a valley, you understand what helping out someone can do for you, it blesses your heart just as much if not more than theirs. Extending a hand to someone can mean, you give them support and encouragement, maybe drive them back home after they walked out, or take them to church. Teach them to manage money, how to pray, about God or a life skill they are lacking, just to name a few.

Have you ever struggled; I mean really struggled? I've been down in the trenches, and with God's loving grace He threw me a lifeline to get out of the pit of sin, over and over, not just once (apparently, I'm a slow learner)! Ever spend too much money on one thing and unable to pay your bills? How about been without food or electricity? Have you been to the trenches? What did it teach you? Or were you like me and had to go back a few times before learning the lesson? Ever had someone come along and get you into trouble? Yes, we make our own choices, but the company we keep plays a huge part in that as well. Caution! Caution!

Have you ever had someone do something to you that was flat out awful? Nobody deserves to be treated that way, or have to go through something terrible, you can't believe it happened, and it left you so scarred. Yea, I been there a few times. You are never alone, for one you have a precious loving Savior who cared enough to take it to the cross, to die for you. Then He put people around your life to extend an arm, reach out that hand and pick you back up when you found yourself stuck in those trenches and pits of life. These people are not just around by accident. God knew how to place us in the families, and groups, and places where we can grow and learn from others around us and our circumstances. We have a Good God! A Loving God!

No matter where you are, where you have been, what you have done, and the not-so-great choices you have made, just remember, it's never too late to change. It's never to late to start over. It's never too late to begin your Fearless Growth® journey.

God's word says...

You may feel trapped by the demands of others and there is just no way to please everyone. To please one is to disappoint another, and this can be frustrating or make us feel trapped or uneasy. Have you ever been caught in a no-win situation? Felt like you just want to run away? We can run but our problems will be right there when we get back, still to be dealt with. Therefore, it is better in these instances when we feel all these demands, pressure, and oppression, to deal with it, not run away or try to ignore it, but get down to the root of where it is coming from and address it head on.

get rid

You were given this life because you were strong enough to live it. God's plan is much better than ours even when it hurts, keep growing.

BECKYMICHEL.COM

"Why is this happening to me? Why do those people insist on doing those awful things, being stubborn, and creating frustration for me no matter how hard I try to be kind, do the right thing, or be the bigger person?" Have you ever felt that way? This could be people you work with, go to class or church with, it can even be friends and family. No matter who or what the experience, no matter how big or small, it is vitally important to either get rid these toxic relationships and behaviors or change them. Sometimes you hear teaching about cutting ties with those who do not serve you on your journey, and while there is much wisdom in this, that's not realistic when it is the people God has bound us together with. In these situations, we must learn to set boundaries and make the kind of changes that allow you to free yourself from any feelings, frustration, or uneasiness they put upon you.

The reality is it's not them "doing" it to you, it's the fact you allow them to. Often times people don't actually realize what it is they are doing, and sometimes unfortunately...they do. You have to remember that when people treat you hatefully or with anger, it's not about you, it is an issue with them. It's the matters they have yet to get honest about and deal with in order to experience some closure, peace, and love. For some this day never comes, for others they might try to deal with these not so pleasant issues but find it's just too hard and settle with being okay with never overcoming what might have them stuck, and that stops growth. As for the rest of us, we sometimes just don't know how to figure it out, or understand the process of the journey. God's grace is so sufficient, and his love and mercy such a BIG gift. When you just don't know, you don't know, it's that simple. We have to learn to be patient and understanding, with love and mercy towards these people, who have yet to figure some things out, like myself. Yea, I'm a prodigal, how about you?

Having said that, I also want to be clear on the fact, God doesn't just expect us to sit on the sideline and put up with a bunch of nonsense continually and intentionally from others. If somebody is doing something to you that is not right in any way, STOP IT! If you don't know how, reach out to someone who can help you, someone you can trust, search for a group or use key words on line to find help, but at all costs however you can, get away from any harmful situation. How many times do we hear someone say I can't tell anyone about this or something bad will happen, or perhaps they are threatening you in some way? If you are in danger of physical abuse, rape, domestic violence or such, it is vitally important to remove yourself from this relationship. If you are experiencing bullying in class, or at the work place, STOP IT! Possibly it's a less serious offense, like being misunderstood by most people or you continually get put down or criticized within your circle, there are ways to release yourself from this toxicity.

Setting boundaries is a nice healthy way to help yourself start experiencing Fearless Growth. Boundaries come in many forms, many various ways. The most important thing to remember when setting boundaries is that you don't build walls in the process.

Once upon a time I done this within my marriage. My husband and I were at a place that things just didn't seem to improve no matter what I would try to do or not do. We just were not able to understand each other, therefor, he was determined not to change. This made it extremely difficult to grow together. The reality of this was that neither of us were taking it to God in the way that we needed to. So finally, at that time, I decided to change some things. For things to change, we must change; so, I learned to set boundaries for both of us. I was no longer going to have unrealistic expectations of my husband, I was no longer willing to accept any critical or negative words, and I would stop allowing little things to affect me. I learned to just let them roll like water off a duck back, and it worked quite well for the most part, other than I put up some massive steel fifty footers. Once those walls are up it can be quite hard to tear them down.

God's word says...

There is no true freedom without repentance. It is a relief to finally give up the weight of our lies and excuses. When we confess our sins, God is faithful and just to forgive us, and remembers them no more. In fact, my God is so big that He removes them as far from us as the east is from the west. Now that is some big love, mercy, grace filled freedom. You no longer need to hang on to the shame or fear that comes with those sins or poor choices. The fear of the Lord is the beginning of wisdom, this scripture helps us understand that to fear God is not to live in fear but to know His greatness. He knows how weak we are and shows us his unfailing love as we grow and fear Him. This is the only fear we should carry. God is like a father to his children, tender and compassionate. Who has received a Jesus whipping besides me? They sure hurt, but are for my own good. It's hard in the moment, but once it passes, I always come out better than I was, because I allowed God to chasten me for my own growth, and I can have peace by remembering joy comes in the morning. It is a choice to either accept God's correction, or not, He doesn't constantly accuse us or remain angry forever. I use to feel God was disappointed in me and there was nothing I could do to change that. I though that when I stumbled or displeased God, I would never be any more than a filthy rag. Then one day I learned while I am nothing without God, Jesus won that victory for me long ago and I can relax about trying to be righteous enough because I never will be and He loves me just the same. I am imperfect and will always be and that's okay, because today I accept it and that's why I need my Jesus! Just my personal gleaning from God's word. Study for yourself.

Some of the things God showed me at that time were so true and so good for my growth. Those good attributes I took away I will mention in a bit, however it was this one thing that remained holding me back no matter how much I was learning and growing and that was the building of those big old massive walls. Not just towards my husband but towards everyone. No more was "Becky" going to allow others to make her feel bad, hurt her feelings, criticize, or come at her. Nope, I no longer was accepting the sticks and stones the people of my world would throw at me. Well, here's the reality, those harsh sticks and stones, those came straight from the enemy, not the people. It took me about 3 days of being totally ticked at everyone around me before God gently said to me, it's not them it's you. While people will take advantage of us, and spitefully use us, it is only because they are being used as a tool of the enemy. The devil has our number, unfortunately he knows what buttons to push on us.

When someone or something steps over one of your boundaries, you don't move the boundary, you move the person or thing.

BECKYMICHEL.COM

God's word says...

A boundary is a limit you personally set. It allows you space and time to process and to remain healthy both mentally and physically. Boundaries can be physical, mental, for your body, in relationships, with your beliefs, heck, even our thoughts must be taken captive. Without personal boundaries, our lives will be messy. Without boundaries you can be led astray by influential people who are eager to control areas of your life that don't belong to them. You can allow yourself to be exposed to temptations that can hurt others because you will cross the line with them and seek to control areas of their lives which are inappropriate for you to do as well. When boundaries are left unset, we cannot grow in the grace and knowledge that God has for us. Remember; your identity in Christ separates you from your old identity in the world. 1 John 4:1-3 helps us identify some areas in our beliefs where we should set boundaries. God's word shows us that if we are a Christian above anything else, a mom, wife, worker, writer, etc., we are first and foremost a Christ follower. This boundary alone separates the old man from the new man. In John, Jesus helped Peter remember where his focus should be, not on what he can't control but what he can. Don't worry about John, and you take care of your own self. We can worry our whole life away focused on things that are out of our control. Hurting others by continually pushing and pulling them to get them to do what we think they should or what we feel is best, which is not at all God's best for either party. This hurts us as well when we allow others to do it to us in return, or at least try to do it to us, and run our lives. God holds me responsible for this. On my judgment day I will not stand with my parents or spouse, I will stand alone, so I better make sure what I am doing is okay with God regardless of anyone else's opinions or personal beliefs.

God showed me how to stand up for myself. He showed me my purpose and while others may not understand it, that's ok, because I came to a place that I now do. The areas He helped me see, stop, and change are what I refer to as my "ridders". The things I started getting rid of. This is where learning to set boundaries became so helpful. Being myself is exactly what God wants of me, to show up exactly as I am, unashamed, authentic, broken, a mess, yet grateful for those places He has brought me out of. To run my very own race. Sometimes I think we get stuck running someone else's, even our spouse's. When we understand who we are in Christ, we can get on a new track, our own track, and that is the exact place God wants us. God showed me I had to change every relationship in my life, yes, every one! This was the process God was walking me through. I begin to change, and while change can be difficult, or we may fear it, you can be sure of these two things; Number one, it's going to happen, regardless if we like it or hate it. Number two, change will be the only factor that will grow us. Growth can only come with change. It is up to you how you will deal with it.

God's word says...

Growing up I did not know or learn about boundaries. When we understand what a boundary is and how to create them and why, it can really take the pressure off from feeling guilt, shame, fear, and a multitude of other unhealthy feels that don't come from God. We are often taught to close ourselves off rather than talking through the pain, problem, or situation. Sometimes I think this is taught naturally as the older generations maybe we're not taught or perhaps never understood matters of communication and were taught that silence is better than speaking. While there is a time to be silent, it doesn't really apply when learning our identity, and communication, or standing up for truth, etc. As I say all the time, if a person doesn't know, they just don't know. But once we become aware, that rule no longer applies and to him that knows to do good and does it not, it is sin. If feelings and emotions are not openly discussed, how would we know how to deal with and process them or how to understand whether those feels or emotions are to help or hurt us, or if they came from God or the devil? Not learning how to deal with our own emotions or how to process pain and uncomfortable feels and situations can really keep us from the growth God had intended for us. Ultimately this hurts us and our own personal growth. Sometimes we also adapt to taking on the pain of others, again, just not being self-aware enough to understand what we are doing, at that point we are not just carrying our baggage around but others as well. By setting healthy boundaries it allows us to guard our hearts as scripture teaches us in proverbs 4:23.

My sister and I were recently chatting about her husband and how he carries himself. He doesn't allow anyone to affect him. If someone tries to attack him, he laughs at them, if they are poking fun at him, he just lets it roll. Literally he doesn't allow anyone to make him feel lesser about himself, or get him in a state of negative self-distress. I just think wow, if only we would all practice this, how much it would help everyone.

Sure, people are going to joke around with you. Maybe even talk to your spouse a little too flirty' or come at your kids while they completely ignore their own when they are doing the same thing. These are all things we don't care for or ever enjoy having to deal with. but will we allow them to get the best of us or learn to confront them when need be, and after that let them roll? Absolutely everyone is going to have a bad day every now and again, heck I come in attack at my family when I don't mean to at all, it just happens sometimes. Or sometimes everyone at my house will misread mom, thinking I am mad or upset with them, when the reality is that I am just cranky for no particular reason. I'm simply having a bad day. Why? Shoot, I don't know! Why do any of us say or do the things we do sometimes? Because we are all human, living in this flesh, this flesh that we must battle on a regular daily basis in order to stay on our course.

Once we learn to get rid of those things, we can take a real hard look at, or come to terms with that is when we advance in the growth process. That's Fearless Growth!

God's word says...

If we are open to allowing others to help us, talk through pain and guide us we can grow and achieve so much more from God's word than if we are closed and decide we don't need help and can do it on our own, this expresses the exact thing we are struggling with...vulnerability. After all these emotional issues are only fixed if we are teachable and willing to change. Maybe you learned to repress unwanted or uncomfortable feelings and allow pain to grow inwardly. Sometimes we think we can discern and dissect it on our own, and while that's quite possible and God is the great physician and a friend that is closer than any brother, and yes, we can take it all to him, he has given us a special gift, other humans! These are friends, family, realities, mentors, cousin's, etc., People to help and encourage us and people for us to help and encourage as well. How many times have I prayed, and got clarity? Many! How many times have I not been able to pray and called on a friend to do so for me? Many! How many times have I talked through a situation or conflict that I just couldn't get clarity on only to immediately see it clearer once I spoke it outward to someone I could trust, or they helped me sort through the facts to get clarity? I don't know about you, but I thank God for these gifts God has placed in and around my life. Yes, we do have God's word, but do we have accountability, conversation, and learning opportunities? I have seen time after time, even in my own life, that there are just some things I cannot do on my own. It's not shameful to need help, nor is it embarrassing. Although Jesus didn't need the help, he used and allowed other people to help him in his ministry, they even traveled with him. Jesus set boundaries, going off by himself, to get alone, in his relationships with individuals, his disciples, getting the rest he needed, all things important to our mental health. All things so important for growth.

get going

Now we come to the exciting and third part of Fearless Growth. Sometimes it's so simple that we completely miss it, like I mentioned in the first chapter of this book. God began pouring Fearless Growth into me over ten years ago, and it didn't come without some massive hills and valleys I had to go through, and there are plenty more where those come from, as I journey on. One of the first things God put in me was words, stories, and versus. I began to write and study what God was showing me. Yes, He was growing me and I had many growing pains. But the one thing I consistently did was, I never stopped. I commenced to learning about opinions versus God's truth, and that God's plan for me and who He wanted me to be wasn't necessarily like others around me, and that was okay…God gave me permission to be me. God puts different things in each of us, different callings, missions, character, personalities, and abilities. Why? To grow the body. The body has a very difficult time growing if it can not come together in unity. If it can not stand to be together, if it is subject to fighting, or being at odds all the time, then how can it grow in grace and knowledge?

I came out of some pretty deep negative self-talk and sabotaging thinking. Yes, I looked happy outwardly, but inside I was a mess…in so many ways. I started simple and began to work on improving my posture, then I worked on how I showed up, and carried myself. I don't mean my physical posture but my values and beliefs. How did God want Becky to show up? Authentically, as myself, only that's not how I lived my life, so I begin to study to show myself approved for the first time ever, and to become confident in who I was. That was the beginning of my Fearless Growth journey.

God's word says...

In order to know how to love others, I had to first understand God's love for me, and know how to love myself. I learned early that love isn't lasting, it comes with conditions. The thing I knew about myself 15 years ago is I could make you like me, because I wanted your approval, I had no voice, and I said what others wanted to hear to avoid rejection. I honestly didn't know who I was outside of my amazing people pleasing skills, and I wanted no part of the shame and guilt that came with saying no, or confrontation, or letting someone down, therefore I was a yes girl, and quite frankly, a fraud, because I didn't understand God's love as I do today. Jesus commands us to love others as we love ourselves, but how can I do this if I don't love me, and how can I love me when I don't even know me. This was all very deep and very new for me, as I had never thought too much about it until God began to help me see issues with myself, my relationships, and where I was in life while moving me towards my purpose. Real love first knows God's love. A wise boundary says I will help myself first, so I am able to help those around me, this means the people pleasing had to stop. Once I can sit with God and know Him and his love, that's when I have understood how to love others.

Real love doesn't feel resentful or make others feel guilty later. I have been guilty of this when I have tried to do God's work on my own or put up with too much and lived as a peacemaker, rather than standing up for myself. Learning not to cast your pearls before swine is super hard for the empathetic person, but an incredibly important lesson.

It is vitally important to get busy to grow. Anytime you are not moving forward, rest assure you are moving backwards, because that is exactly what being stuck means. Everyone gets stuck from time to time, but the important thing is that you continue to try and to learn and grow from those times. Even when you don't understand them, like not getting cooked in the squat.

How we move forward from every situation in life determines an outcome which is either good or bad. How will you deal with and grow from your outcomes? The third part of growing Fearlessly is to simply get going with the things God shows you about yourself. It's taking those not so pleasant dreary situations, struggles, and issues we have had, and making sunshine out of them. This is a process and can be a challenge. It definitely takes some time.

The really great part is that you can start over today, right now, you can start the journey of Fearless Growth® right there in that chair, or car, or room, wherever you are. Nobody is stopping you; nobody is in charge of you, except you. To "get going" is for you to ask God to help you, teach you, show you, and He will. Begin to make changes, and see yourself now. The hardest person to see is me, it's so easy to point at everyone else, but me, that's not so enjoyable or easy.

God's word says...

When Jesus went to the pool of Bethesda in John chapter 5, He seen a sick many laying there who had been ill for a long time and Jesus asked him, would you like to get well?" This is a very important question, for some people do not truly want help, the truth or want to grow because it's easier to just stay where they are. There is wisdom in an ask. Then we have God's mercy when we don't deserve it, so while the man was making excuses, he was healed. Jesus told him to help himself in that moment as well, get up and get your mat and walk. The man was willing to help himself. Am I willing to do some work to get better? Are you? I have learned to ask lots of questions in order to see where people really are. Sometimes this helps others see themselves, since I am of course the hardest person to see. As I see myself through God's lens I can began to believe what His words says about me.

For I am fearfully and wonderfully made and marvelous are thy works. Psalm 139:14

I am chosen and royalty! I am a child of the King! I can live free because I am called out of the darkness into His marvelous light. I have God's permission to be bold and set boundaries for my protection. 1 Peter 2:9 & Romans 8:29

I am His workmanship, created in God's image. Ephesians 2:10 & Genesis 1:27

I am confident in God and when I feel alone, He will never abandon me. I am confident that when I get knocked down, God is helping me back up. I may be perplexed, but not in despair 2 Corinthians 4:8,9 & Philippians 1:6

Getting uncomfortable is the third and final part to growth. It's not easy to be uncomfortable, its…well uncomfortable. I can't tell you how many times my immediate family, kids, parents, siblings, have been frustrated with me. Why? Because I've made life so uncomfortable sometimes! Yep, it was a big pain, I've been a big pain. Why would anyone want to have uncomfortable conversations? Because growth comes when I get outside my comfort zone, and when I am willing to have honest conversations. Does it suck, you bet it does. Why would anyone do that? Because there is joy in the journey when you learn to submit. Remember, the process becomes priceless, because we are able to get ourselves out of our own way. I've done it for me and I've done it for my family at times when I felt led by God. You can ask them how much they have been frustrated with me for turning around and doing the exact thing I told them not to do, and I'm certain they would say many! That's what makes me a prodigal, not a hypocrite. Which by the way, come on now, who isn't a hypocrite? Who is willing to face the fear head on in order to get to new ground, or a new level, and who's not? That is what separates the prodigal from the religious and non-caring hypocritical crowds.

God's word says...

I am confident and I have confidence in knowing that God knew me in my mother's womb, before I was born, and set me apart and chose me for such a time as this. I have confidence that I have already won a victory over my struggles and battles, because the Spirit who lives in me is greater than the spirit who lives in the world. God tells me I am precious to Him, I am honored, and loved by Him. Because of the victory through and in Him I have no obligation to do what my sinful nature urges me to do, and that is totally praise worthy. Romans 8:12, Isaiah 43:4, 1 John 4:4, Jeremiah 1:5

I am bought by the blood, I have freedom, and can rest in God's unconditional love for me. I am confident in who I am and am not trying to win the approval of people any longer, PRAISE JESUS!

What are you doing right now that promotes change and growth in your life? These things must be intentional. Waking up earlier, going to bed earlier, working out, having a routine, setting boundaries, reading God's instruction manual, (The Bible), filling up with good food, versus awful food. I believe there is a balance to everything. If you are watching too much TV or playing every weekend but not attending service with the church body yet you say you are a believer, somewhere you are off balance. I call this your "Joy Flow". Of course, we are going to find entertainment Movies, playing around, fun, fun, fun, but when we leave out work, and God, and good wholesome food, there will not be growth. By food I not only mean what you put in your mouth, which is indeed important. But I'm talking about what you read, watch, where you go, and who you spend your time with. You can't just plant a seed, walk away and expect it to grow. You must prepare the ground, plant, water, cultivate it, and then growth can take place. Change is always required in some area, and often times several areas to balance out that Joy Flow. What changes can you make today to balance out your life?

God's word says...

I know that God doesn't want me to have fear, and that I am more valuable to Him than the sparrows. I can change because God has given me the ability to renew my thoughts and attitude. The same power that rose Jesus from the grave lives in me. He gives me strength and cares about me, and because of this, I can do all things through Him. I have love because He first loved me. He has special plans for me, a good future, hope, with purpose and a vision. I am allowed to dream big, as God guides me in the plan he has for Becky. I am to be strong and courageous, and not discouraged because He is always with me and nothing can separate me from His love. He gives me inner strength through his spirit and empowers me to show up and be who He calls me to.

I am Christ's ambassador and His heir and he calls me by my name, I am so thankful, because Satan calls me by my sins.

Without understanding who we are in Christ, we will never come fully alive to who He has created us to be. It is impossible to give love that you don't have.

If you have read through this study guide and feel you would benefit from the entire Fearless Growth™ series, look me up on Amazon.com or visit me on my website www.BeckyMichel.com or www.growwithbecky.com . If you would like to do group coaching with me, visit me via my website or shoot me an email at Becky@BeckyMichel.com. So now come on! Get real, get rid, and get going. Start today, don't wait until it's too late!

Much love, Becky

Fear
joshua 1:9
Weary
matthew 11:28
Hope
psalm 42:5
Forgivness
1 john 1:9
Anxious
1 peter 5:7
Strength
phillip 4:13
psalm 34:17
Helpless
Anger
Eph 4:26-27
psalm 27:14
Waiting
john 14:27
Peace
psalm 27:14
Waiting
duter 31:6
Courage
let go
and let
God
FEARLESS GROWTH

God's word says...

It's so true what Paul says in Romans 8:28, that all things work together for good to those who love God, and are called according to His purpose. Who besides me is completely unqualified to do what God has called me to and where he has put me? Satan knows my vice and with which I struggle, so it doesn't take him long to interfere with my purpose, which is why I must run when I am tempted to lose focus, yep guilty again. Satan's goal is to keep us away from God and to keep us from fulfilling the plan and purpose God has for us both while we are here on earth, and the afterlife. If you have been inspired or encouraged by this study guide, I encourage you to continue with the three set Fearless Growth books. I want to personally encourage you to ask God for help every day, seek to know His unlimited power, and learn of His unchanging love for you so that you can learn how to love yourself, others, and have confidence in your identity so that you can Fearlessly Grow in the grace and knowledge of our Lord. Dear friend, don't lose heart. God loves and needs you. I see you, and I want to celebrate your value!

IF YOU SEE SOMEONE FALLING BEHIND, WALK BESIDE THEM.

IF YOU SEE SOMEONE BEING IGNORED, FIND A WAY TO INCLUDE THEM.

ALWAYS REMIND PEOPLE OF THEIR WORTH. ONE SMALL ACT COULD MEAN THE WORLD TO SOMEONE.

BECKYMICHEL.COM

HELP SOMEONE ELSE EVEN IF NO ONE IS HELPING YOU.

BECKYMICHEL.COM

Quotes...

The following is a collection of Bex Q's (Quotes by Becky):

"Comparison is the thief of joy – Don't be afraid to be you"

"Sometimes you just need someone to hold the light for you, other times you need to hold it for someone else"

"Don't compare yourself to others, compare yourself to the you from yesterday"

"I am not what has happened to me. I am what I choose to become because of it"

"Note to self: Stop pleasing people and start pleasing God"

"The key to success looks different to everyone. But the key to failure will result from trying to please everyone"

"I use to coach confidence; one common factor I seen was that confidence is silent but insecurities are loud"

"Nothing makes a woman more beautiful than confidence"

"93% of people who quit too soon are employed by the 3% that never give up"

"Be yourself. Don't wait for approval"

"I'm still standing"

"Confidence is strength"

"How you finish is what matters"

"Step out of your comfort zone"

"Confidence is not a trait, it must be learned and practiced"

"Confidence can be practiced and learned like any skill"

"You wouldn't worry so much about what others think about you if you realize how little they do"

"Confidence comes from not always being right, but not fearing to be wrong"

"Confidence will always drive away doubt"

"Focus forward with forgiveness"

"Happiness doesn't bring grattitude, gratitude brings happiness"

"Today…Have Fun!"

Notes...

Notes...

Notes...

Notes...

Notes...

Notes...

54

Notes...

Notes...

Notes...

Notes...

Notes...

Notes...

Notes...

Notes...

62

Notes...

     Becky Michel

Notes...

64

Notes...

65

Notes...

Notes...

Notes...

Notes...

Notes...

Notes...

Notes...

Notes...

Notes...

Notes...

You are allowed to set
boundaries for people who
behave in ways that harm you!
(mentally, emotionally, physically)

BECKYMICHEL.COM

Cutting ties with someone who
continues to hurt you isn't
enough. You must cut ties with
the version of you who allowed
that to continue for as long as it
did.

BECKYMICHEL.COM

Abuse...

First, I am not a psychologist or do I want you to blindly follow anything I or anyone else says without prayerfully seeking God's word and wisdom. I'm simply sharing with you the things I have learned by studying the Bible in the attempt to deal with my own personal situations regarding these types of behaviors and people, including myself.

Over the years I have noticed a rise in silent emotional and psychological abuse. It is time to address it in the church. Being in submission to your husbands and husbands loving their wives goes much deeper than a mindset of authority to obedience, and opening a car door or cooking a meal.

Mental and emotional health needs to be addressed more than ever in the world we live. As life gets busier, more and more people are hurting but unsure where to turn to for help. As the church tries to help them, it struggles because of its own fragile state. The church does not understand abuse or the dynamics of pain and love that shadow it. We have become so self-centered and judgmental that the focus is not on loving the lost, broken, and hurting to Jesus but rather "fixing" them in our own sight. We don't even know what we need, so how can we possibly know what someone else might need or have the mental capacity to work on them when we do not know how to work on ourselves. How can we love others as Christ loves us, if we can't even love ourself, or even truly understand His love for us?

Therefore, I feel the need to address a very small piece of abuse here, and provide a few resources.

What is abuse? (In my own words) When someone treats you in any way that is of unequal respect or value to gain a benefit of some sort.

Usually, the goal is for control. Abuse can come in many forms such as: domestic violence, physical, verbal, psychological, emotional, mental, financial, spiritual, injury, assault, violation, rape, sexual, unjust practices, cultural, racial, religious, crimes, animal cruelty, antiquated beliefs about roles of women and men in relationships, possessiveness, impulsiveness, bad temper, extreme controlling behavior, or other types of aggression. A few examples of abuse are:

- Monitoring and controlling another person's behavior, such as who they spend time with, how they spend money, where they go, etc.

- Threatening a person's safety, property, or loved ones.

- Isolating or attempting to isolate a person from family, friends, and acquaintances, or people in general.

- Belittling, shaming, humiliating

- Extreme jealousy, accusations, and paranoia

- Delivering constant criticism -This starts very small as a person judges your perspective without trying to understand it. They rely on blame rather than improvement, regarding the other person as inferior. They sometimes tell others how to feel in attempts to be helpful.

- Regular ridicule, teasing, and or, "making fun of"

- Silence and yelling are both forms of abuse if the abuser is using them for their gain. Both are signs of mental distress. Neither silent treatment, or harsh commands are acceptable types of communication.

- Making acceptance or care conditional on another person's choices. This is a conditional love. "I love you only when you do this. I do this for you because you do this for me."

- Refusing to allow a person to spend time alone

- Disturbing a person's professional or personal goals

- Instilling self-doubt and worthlessness

- Gaslighting: making a person question their competence and even their basic perceptual experiences.

Cycle of Abuse

1 Tensions Building
Tensions increase, breakdown of communication, victim becomes fearful and feels the need to placate the abuser.

4 Calm
Incident is "forgotten." No abuse is taking place. The "honeymoon" phase.

2 Incident
Verbal, emotional, and physical abuse. Anger, blaming, arguing. Threats. Intimidation.

3 Reconciliation
Abuser apologizes, gives excuses, blames the victim, denies the abuse occured, or says it wasn't as bad as the victim claims.

How do I know if it's abuse or just someone who can't control their emotions or reactors?

Ask yourself these questions and remember if something doesn't feel right, it usually is not.

- Do I feel mutual respect from this person?

- Do I feel taken advantage of by this person?

- Does this person need things to go their way or else they get upset?

- Do I ever feel fear of any kind when I am around them?

- In what way does this person get upset, and what emotions and feelings do they show when they are upset?

Abusive people believe they have the right to control and restrict their partners' lives, and or, the lives of others. They don't understand boundaries. They have an unhealthy mindset of where they end and the other person begins. They see their spouse/child/friend, as an extension of themselves, therefore that person is not entitled to have any boundaries. The lack of distance means a person is subject to whatever the abuser decides. So many times, an abuser lives in fear.

People who act and react out of fear tend to use their emotions as justifications for why another person needs to do what is demanded of them. Almost as though the fear is so powerful that nothing else matters except the need to subside it, being…another person's obedience.

People who are abusive or are prone to abusive behaviors often lack empathy, as it is far easier to abuse someone you have no care about. These types of people like to be in charge. They utilize inefficient means of dominance such as bullying or intimidation. While forced control can be quickly executed, it does not have lasting qualities.

I have seen such types of abuse in adult children and parent relationships, in the church, the workplace, and in politics to name a few.

Abusers have a root issue that they have never addressed, which is why they continue to project these behaviors.

Most often abusers believe their feelings and needs should come first, which comes from feelings of "I deserve". That mindset can come from being lifted in pride and overly confident or because they enjoy exerting power that abuse gives them.

Some abusers have some sort of disorder or mental health issues, they like to gain personal pleasure from hurting others. Some abused themselves, acting out of their dysfunctional behaviors towards others, as it was done unto them.

Often, they have anger issues, which come from insecurities. Of course, we all have some insecurities, but abusers are unwilling to search out their own insecurities and address them, which typically must be done with the help of someone else like a third party.

Unmanaged rage produces abusive behavior. Sometimes insecurities are brought on by traumatic events. Unresolved trauma sparks anger when triggered. Possibly an abuser grew up with an addict. An addict blames others for their problems, and this list can go on and on without end. This is just my searching out and learning of abuse and abusive traits.

Next Step

- Prayerfully consider character qualities as you digest this information.

- Someone who is not an actual abuser but has just developed some bad habits will be willing to work on themselves.

- They will be willing to give you mutual respect as you communicate to them about how you feel.

- They will respect the boundaries you set.

- They would be happy to do whatever you need to feel better, whether that means seeking council, taking a class, going to anger management, or sitting down with trusted sources, etc., even if they don't believe in what it is you need.

- They will be more than willing to put effort into doing the work because they love you.

- Mention your concerns to your spouse or the "possible abuser", and ask if you can discuss the matter with them. Your first red flag is if they become immediately defensive or angry. Many times, people of an abusive nature carry so much pride they are unable to acknowledge that others have mentioned or seen the same behavior in them that you are addressing.

Do I go back to them and or make restitution with this person? Every situation is different and must be prayerfully dissected and dealt with. A few questions I would have for you is

1. have you communicated your feelings directly to this person?

2. In my personal experience, I asked each of my abusers for a very specific thing, not hard, just requiring humility and mutual respect, which none of them were willing to do or show.

Communicate exactly what you need for the situation to be fixed or better, healing to take place, adjustments, etc. If they completely disregard your request or put you off, like "ignoring, or "I will do it later", this is another red flag. I would put a date to your request. If I had it to do over again this is the thing I would have added as I did one of the times, to get on with life and out of the relationship sooner.

About Restitution...

1. If God clearly or precisely tells you to stop and gives you permission to move on, cut ties, etc. These are often cases that are toxic not only to you but to your children. These are extreme cases of physical, sexual, or abuse that endangers you. Or the simple fact that this person is not ready to self-examine, and meet you with mutual respect. If this is the case and you are certain you heard from God…obey!

2. You must acknowledge if making restitution would be the best thing, or simply closing that door and moving on when considering what action to take. How many times have I heard of someone being sexually abused because the mother was fearful and just allowed it to happen to her daughter? Consider what the root issue is and if it is something you can take care of yourself.

3. If you have asked this person, even once and they did not respect you enough to listen or care about your feelings or request, do you foresee them changing if you were to restore the relationship with them?

I restored the relationship with my husband who, yes was an abuser to me, because he FINALLY (upon signing a contract) acknowledged that I was serious and meant business this time. I had a plan and I was sticking to it. It wasn't that he was a bad person at all. In fact, he is an amazing person, very caring, with a kind loving heart, it was just that he had some very toxic behaviors and he was allowed to demonstrate them for so long that the thought of change was fearful and shameful.

Pride will always say, don't yield because you will appear weak. When truly it is just the opposite, Jesus wants us to come to Him, broken, in our mess. Humility is not weakness it is meekness. It was only when my husband realized his need for growth and change that our relationship began to improve, twenty years later. You can love someone to death, kill them with kindness, and pray your heart out for them, but if they will never see themselves for truly where they are at, all the love, kindness, and prayers in the world won't help them. They must humbly come to Jesus with a hungry spirit for change.

"Just because we know something doesn't mean it's going to stop us"
– Jeff Michel

4. This is the only way that I personally would restore relationships with any of my abusers. If they were to come to me with a truly changed heart. I would have a plan in place and there would be a process with witnesses and the restoration would have new boundaries. I have forgiven each of them, but forgiveness is not for the other person it is for you and it does not mean we go break bread and go back to how things were. What would that accomplish, nothing for either of you? However, truth and boundaries will.

Power and Control Wheel

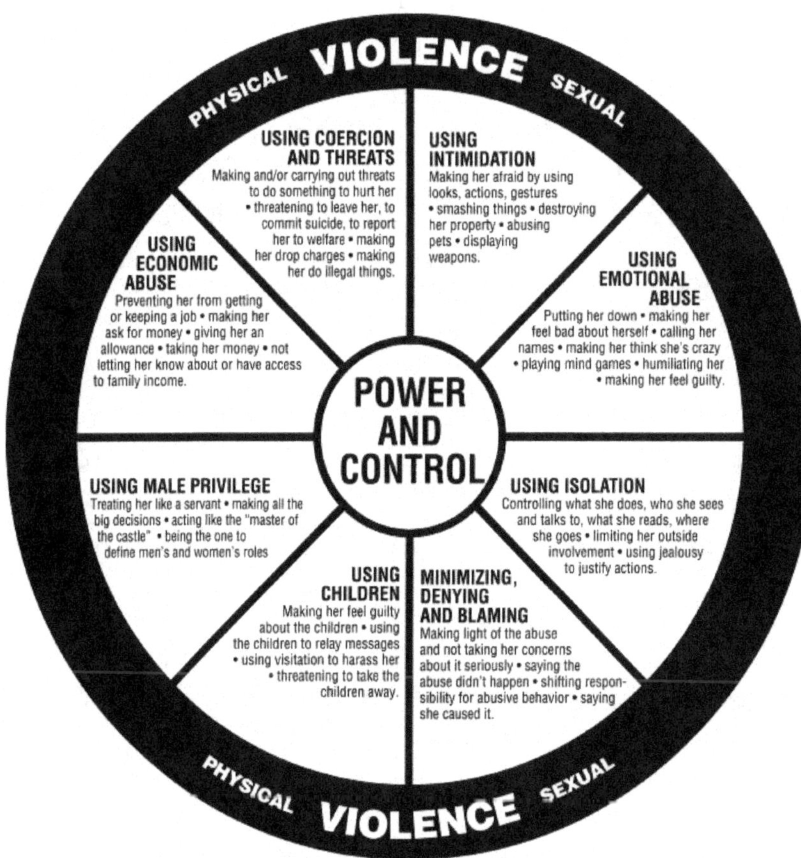

What is a narcissist?

A narcissist is described as a person who has an excessive interest in or admiration of themselves. Essentially someone who is extremely self-centered, simply put, and certain traits, betray their self-centeredness. They have an extreme, kind of a splendid view of their self-importance, they are the center of the universe. Often you won't see this about them at first, because they tend to come across as very charming and maybe even caring people, intelligent, but beneath the surface, once you get to know them, you realize that they think that they're really, really, really important. Basically, they're living in a sort of fantasy world where everybody else is expendable, except for them.

My personal response to that attitude is: that nobody is expendable, and pride goes before a fall. God teaches us humility by disciplining us when we allow pride to get hold of us. And the narcissist is definitely in that category, sadly they just don't tend to learn. When they do fall, it's everyone else's fault, it's never their fault, they're always the victim.

People who are soft-hearted and empathetic, tend to fall victim to the narcissists as they are easy to blame. If you were involved in any of their issues in any way, they can successfully convince you that, "you're the whole problem here".

You may find them throwing fits when faced with disappointments or when they don't get their way. This is usually with rage, not normal anger, but an "everyone's walking on eggshells around them" type of anger because you just never know when they are going to blow. You can see it on their face, in their demeanor, by clenched fists, a resting irate face, a raised voice, and so forth.

Oddly enough, as fast as they can turn it on, they can turn it off. And they go right back into that charming mode again and it's like it never happened. The people who are their victims, within their sphere of influence, are left wondering what just happened? Did I see that rightly? Is something wrong with me? This can produce many months, years, or even decades of questioning yourself about every little thing that happens in life, wondering if you are wrong about everything, especially if this is someone you lived with like a parent or spouse.

The narcissist is often a great gas lighter, which means they're causing you to question yourself. Your perceptions can't be right, because their perceptions are right, and with this can come a lot of manipulation and mind games. It's important to realize the chances of them changing are slim, but the only way it will truly happen is through God. I had to educate myself on gaslighting as I spent half my life questioning if I was the issue when I was not. That's not to say I don't have problems or can be a pain, because I certainly can, but I'm simply stating what comes along with narcissistic behaviors.

How can you know if someone in your life is a narcissist? Maybe you are dealing with a person who is a narcissist and has all the characteristics of it, but they say they are a believer. If they can't have healthy relationships with others, how do they have a relationship with God?

A narcissist will not think twice about turning anyone against you whom they feel is a threat to them. They will often be jealous of people who admire you, in mutual relationships, they will go after anyone necessary to change their view of you. And of course, they can't go against you openly, it must be done in secret. With that being said, they will say many nice things about you to the mutual friend/family, but once they've won the confidence of your friend/family, they will say, "I think you should know this about Becky." They began to plant seeds in the minds of people that trust them. Then you discover your friends and family are avoiding you because the narcissist has turned them against you. They lift themselves up by putting you down. Because of their position in your life, you don't realize the damage that they're doing behind the scenes.

Ask yourself the following questions regarding the person you are wondering about:

- Have I ever left their presence and questioned myself or my perspective after a conversation with them? (Example: I know I heard what I heard, saw what I saw, felt what I felt, but after that conversation with them, now I'm not so sure? In fact, I almost feel bad for even saying anything at all now or am starting to wonder if I have a problem with lying or not seeing myself as they say I do.)

- Has the above happened more than once with this person?

- Have you ever felt like they were attacking or making fun of you in public to look or feel better about themselves?

- Possibly the number one question is, have I seen growth and change for the better since I have known them? Have they shown new fruit, and don't do these above things as much, or seem to try to fix their bad behavior, even if they don't speak of it?

What should you do if you find yourself victimized by a narcissist? In my personal opinion, if they are truly a narcissist, you are fighting a losing battle now because if your friends or family have bought into the lies, there is no way of them buying who comes to them second. Second is too late without God's intervention, and that depends on the person at hand.

If they were a true friend or loved you, they would've come and talked to you about it instead of only listening to one side and forming an opinion. I have personally experienced this from the victim's side. There is nothing you can say or do at this point.

I have observed a personal situation where someone I love has bought into the manipulation and lies of the narcissist and now must continue to do as told or they lose their status, money, inheritance, friendship, etc.

This is such a work of the enemy and nobody should bow down to this type of fake love or behavior. This is not unconditional love or a good friend. If you "must do things" to keep someone happy or the other person being kind to you, you need to step back for a moment. Take inventory of where you are and what is going on in this relationship. Do you really enjoy this relationship? Does it fill you with life, love, and joy? Or are you constantly sweating and stressing about what this person is bringing to the table?

A few examples:

- (Other relationships in your life are suffering like, "I can't be friends with Becky, because Joe will find out and Joe is my bookkeeper, and will turn me into the IRS", I know this because he has jokingly mentioned it, and I saw him do it to someone once. "So, I guess I won't be friends with Becky now".

- "I'm going to have to stay away from Becky because she keeps telling me things, I am certain to be true about Aunt Lola, but Aunt Lola gives me amazing gifts and sometimes money, and she helps my family so much. Gosh, I don't feel I could confront Aunt Lola as she will get angry and I know this. So even though Becky is probably right because I can see these toxic qualities in Aunt Lola, and Becky never puts stipulations on her kindness and doesn't criticize and attack me like Aunt Lola, I just really need Aunt Lola in my life. I guess I will just leave Becky alone."

- "I suppose I will close the door on my relationship with Becky because Grandma just doesn't like her writing about her personal true-life experiences and has told her countless times to stop, but she's not stopping. Grandma says it makes our family name look bad, but Becky said she felt God is in complete control, and prayerfully seeks to say what He wants to be said with love. However, I don't know why Becky is so inconsiderate of Grandma. After all, it is her grandmother for heaven's sake. Since Becky is being stupid and causing all these problems, Grandma is now leaving me her farm when she dies, so guess I'll do whatever I need to be the golden grandkid."

For me personally, there is no amount of money you could pay me to put up with this behavior anymore. Friends that aren't worth having are people who will listen to rumors, slander, or lies against you without questioning or understanding both sides before assuming. Sadly, this leaves you to consider is this a friend worth striving to keep? Because they believed a lie about me, they're not even willing to listen to facts or examine the truth. They feel like I'm attacking them because I'm challenging their viewpoint. Are these real friends that I want to fight to keep? They're probably not. So let them go. Getting a narcissist out of your life is sometimes all you can do.

As Jesus instructs us to preach the gospel to people even if they are not going to receive it, it's still our responsibility to tell people the truth because then they're held accountable for it.

If the narcissist knows you're coming to confront him or her, they'll find an excuse not to meet with you. And if they do meet with you and you are at loggerheads, the narcissist would never agree to follow the biblical principles of reconciliation, of getting one or two to come with you and mediate. Nor will they do anything you suggest because they must call the shots and suggestions.

My heart goes out to anyone who's been through this type of relationship dealings.

1 Corinthians 7: 15 tells us that if an unbeliever can't live with you in peace, then let them live without you.

How to Biblically deal with a narcissist.

- See the narcissist for who they are.

Something has happened in their past, they are wounded or have been deeply afflicted by something or someone.

- Stand your ground.

Don't make exceptions or excuses for them. Continuing to put up with unacceptable behavior simply because your desire for them to be better is so strong does not serve them or you.

- Deescalate the situation if you're being attacked.

Step back, take a minute and access your feelings about this. Do you feel uneasy or tense? Often if we feel something isn't right, it is our intuition telling us to flee or set boundaries. Sometimes simply talking through a situation out loud with someone you can trust is all that is needed to gain a more accurate perspective.

- Set boundaries.

Boundaries are for your protection, not theirs. Once someone shows you their true colors it is important to deescalate the situation and see if they have your best interest at hand or their own. Do they respect you as a person? If your answered no to these, it's time to set boundaries.

- Save your energy for things you can change.

No matter how strong our desire to see someone change, the reality is that unless they want to change, they won't. Instead of focusing on that person, focus on helping yourself grow into a better version through this situation.

- Keep your own values intact.

Never lower a bar you have already set because someone is pushing at you with their values, ways, and needs while disregarding yours. Once you realize you are dealing with a narcissist you must become consciously aware when in their presence. They jump on someone who is unguarded before you even know it's happening.

- Pray to maintain your strength.

It takes a lot of courage, strength, and obedience to stand up to someone, especially if it is family or someone God has specifically instructed you to stand up to. To do it with love and forgiveness is not something that can be done in the flesh. Anything we do in life should be done prayerfully if we want a personal relationship with God.

Some studies suggest that narcissism is a psychological condition resulting from excessive pride. Pride is something to be cautious of both yourself and others.

Nehemiah 8:10
Proverbs 25:26
Proverbs 4:23
Proverbs 6:16-17
Matthew 27:12 silence
1 Corinthians 13 verse 4 says; "Love is not rude.

Sometimes a person can go years with simply a vague feeling that something is wrong. Anyone can be a victim or offender of abuse, regardless of their gender. If you didn't grow up with examples of healthy and loving relationships, especially from your parents, abuse might appear completely normal to you.

Your abuser may say they love you, spend time with you and or your family, take you out to dinner, or shopping, but then threaten you, lie to you, ignore you, or act inappropriate with you, all almost always done in private/secret. Most people see this person as a great person, an upright citizen, probably goes to church, charming, they may even express how much they care about you to other people or even convinced others that you are actually the abuser and they are the victim or trying to help you change.

Your mind may start playing tricks on you. For example: "They must be having a bad day", "I had to have misunderstood the nature of their intent, actions, or behavior because they love me and would not intentionally hurt me. "Am I just being dramatic or imagining that?" Or in some cases the victim even has the mentality of "maybe they are right about me, and I deserve this treatment." And these become the distorted lenses through which you view an abusive relationship.

What type of behaviors classify as bad or abusive behaviors?

Often the church does not talk about such sensitive topics, as abuse, sexuality, addictions, anger, dealing with emotions, love, respect, and how to set boundaries for your mental health. Little lone how to communicate and disciple people with these issues or teach them to do such things. These are too sensitive, too challenging to deal with, so we just leave them alone, then what happens? Much of the above! Because we don't have the hard conversations, these things will become a struggle and have become a struggle for many Christians.

Gaslighting (making someone question reality) can be done through a big lie or several small lies.

Triangulation (pitting people against each other) Examples are: Abuser tells your sibling that you are a horrible person. At the same time, they are charming the sibling while convincing other people you are crazy, have mental issues, etc. They will turn others against you in an attempt to keep you in isolation.

Apologies (Abusers can apologize like pros but they do not mean it). They will do whatever is necessary at the moment to appease you but they will not change nor do they seek true personal growth. This can often feel like a hopeful emotional rollercoaster as you think "oh they are having a change of heart" but get disappointed time and time again when you see nothing changes.

Deflecting (Turning things around on you) An abuser will often say that you are abusive in the exact ways they are. If you try to tell them you feel hurt, mistreated, ignored, disregarded, disrespected, or unloved by them, you will suddenly find yourself apologizing to them and comforting their feelings while yours go unattended. As I mentioned above, you may even leave them feeling bad for even mentioning anything which adds to your inner affliction. This behavior is wrong on so many levels.

Blame (You get blamed for your abusers' actions) If they yell at or cuss you, you deserve it. Everything is your fault. You get punished because you should be able to control your emotions. The abuser will never take responsibility for their actions or even partial responsibility.

Minimization (You are dramatizing this) Instead of caring for you they will convince you what they did or said was best for you and was not wrong in any way. They will have you questioning yourself.

Here I have composed a ton of abusive actions and behaviors:

Pushing, slapping, shaking, punching, hitting, scratching, kicking, holding someone down, throwing things at or in your direction, destroying your personal property, breaking things, punching holes in the wall, throwing things, interfering with you while driving. Pushing their hand against you. Covering your mouth or nose, squeezing you, or cutting off air supply. Grabbing your face so you must look at them. Using a weapon or threatening to use a weapon. Threatening to leave you, divorce you, harm you, get back at you, etc. Blocking a doorway so you can't leave, not letting you use the phone, leave the house, talk to people, etc. Insulting, name calling, coitizing or embarrassing you in public. Telling you no one else will ever love you, you are worthless or useless. Telling you what to do, how to do it, controlling you, where you go, who you can and cannot see and what to wear. Not trusting you, being jealous, accusing you of cheating. Constantly checking up on you. Reading emails, texts, DMs, or social media messages. Stealing your passwords or forcing you to give them information, or so what they want or need you to. Not letting you make your own decisions. Getting mad if you get a text from someone else, if you don't respond right away or spend time with other people. Telling you that you are the reason they are abusive or act as they do. Abandoning you at a store or on the side of the road. Reminding you of their superiority, and how they can hurt you or have other people hurt you. Making you feel guilty about ta decision you made or something you did or said. Threatening to harm you, or commit suicide. Starting rumors or threatening to start rumors. Threatening to expose your secrets or private photos. Refusing to listen to you, or care about your feelings even in the least. Telling you that you are overacting, telling you that you are not remember things correctly or that you made things up, or are a liar. Making you feel bad about being upset, constantly changing the subject, or not letting you talk. Keeping you from seeing your friends and family. Only wanting you to hang out with them. Getting annoyed or upset when you spend time on the phone or with other people or with work. Trying to move you far away from your support system. Telling you your friends, or family don't understand your relationship dynamics. They say things like "if you really loved me, you'd want to…", using intimidation, using looks, actions, and gestures to scare you. Standing in a doorway or otherwise resulting to not let you leave. Displaying weapons, driving recklessly, threatening to crash the car, threatening if you tell anyone or call the police something bad will happen. Following you around, stalking you using spoofing apps to call you so they show up as a different person. Constantly calling or texting, sending unwanted letters cards, emails, or gifts. Tracking your location. Being aggressive or excessively jealous, calling others about you, such as coworkers, friends, boss, family. Forcing you to do things you don't want to or make you feel uncomfortable. Withholding money or financial abuse, abusing pets, animals, and animal cruelty. Forcing you to be physical in any way or have sex. Making you feel guilty if you say you don't want to or that's not what wives or girlfriends do, if you do this, I'll do that. Unwanted kissing or touching, knowingly exposing you to HIV, STD's, etc. Forcing you to use or not use birth control, or have a baby, or terminate a pregnancy. Encouraging and giving you drugs or alcohol so that you have less control of your ability to stay in control. Forcing you to have sex with others or forcing you to watch porn. Sending you texts and pictures that are meant to hurt you. Harassing you.

When do I seek help and how?

Upon immediate realization that you are in an abusive situation. The longer you wait to address it or put it off the worse it will become and harder it will be to stop or get out of.

The power and control wheel was developed by the domestic abuse intervention project in Duluth, MN. The abusive behavior it depicts can happen to anyone of any gender and any age. The wheel serves as a diagram of tactics that an abusive person uses to keep their victims in a relationship and or to keep them quiet as they continue to do as they wish. Of course, not all relationships are the same and abuse can never be summarized in just a single diagram, but the power and control wheel presents a useful lens through which to examine domestic violence.

You may be feeling depressed, lonely, tired, anxious, or confused. You need healthy people around you. People who can speak truth, life, and love into you. Create a safety plan that fits your situation. This may be where you will need to sit down with a trusted source. I personally did this myself. I was not able to think clearly, however a trusted friend helped me sift and sort through the details in order to create a plan of action and it worked impeccably. Know where you are going to get help. Establish the people, places, and resources that are safe.

Boundaries...

The best resource I have found for learning about boundaries is the book "Boundaries" by Dr. Henry Cloud & Dr. John Townsend. If you don't own it, you should!

- **What are boundaries?**

Embarrassingly, your abuser was drawn to you because of your qualities. It may be difficult for you to even admit to yourself that you were abused. This can make you feel weak, dumb, or inferior. But that's not who God says you are. Abusers prey on people who are kind, caring, nurturing, and real. You were not abused because you deserved it. The following are areas having healthy boundaries that can best serve you on your Fearless Growth journey.

Physical, sexual, emotional, mental, spiritual, religious, financial, material, time, and non-negotiable boundaries. Boundaries are a way to help you recognize where one person ends and another begins. They help you define the golden rule. How I want to be treated by others and what I am comfortable with.

- **Are having boundaries biblical?**

Many people will feel like they have no support from friends or family. They may feel alone and isolated. It can feel challenging and painful to rebuild relationships and life for yourself as a victim. Wise council, counseling, and supportive safe spaces and people can be extremely helpful. Releasing trauma, pain, and feelings are a huge part of the healing and growth journey. For God has not given us a spirit of fear but of power, love, and a sound mind. Along with all abuse comes fears, and spirits of fear, weakness, messed up minds, thinking and so forth. God's word tells us to love one another. When we do these three things, live free, take responsibility for ourselves and our freedom, and love God and people, then life including marriage can be great! Where the spirit of the Lord is there is liberty. Many times, Jesus answered with silence or bold statements and gestures. When we do not come together, as a team, in a joint effort the entire marriage is incorrect. Husbands love your wives as Christ loved the church, does not mean being the head honcho leader who controls and keeps tabs on the wife, and she is to submit. Wives submitting yourselves to your husband does not mean to subjecting yourself to his authority. A wife was created to be his help meet. The definition of a help meat is a helpful partner. The definition of partner is a pair engaging in the same activity. If you read your bible or go to church and your spouse doesn't, you are not functioning as a team or engaging in the same activity. If you discipline your children in this way and your spouse, does it in another way, again, not a team. If you feel strongly about X, and they feel strongly about Y, and you are unwilling to compromise, still, not functioning as a team or helpful partner. When we love God and love people without an ulterior motive, bitterness, without insecurities, fear, expectations, or baggage from the past, because we have given it to God, it allows us to just love, as we are commanded to. In return, we are free, as we don't need to worry or take care of anyone else, just ourself. A husband is a protector of his wife, this means mentally and emotionally, not just getting out the big guns! When a wife feels safe, she can confide in him, and he in her. If this intimate connection never happens, are we living as the Bible instructs?

I will share a personal example here, in our beginning years of marriage my husband Jeff would say he was my umbrella of protection and forbid me to do some things, even if it was with family. It doesn't matter what they were. At first, he needed to physically see where I was at all times or be with me. Little did I know he had undealt with insecurity issues, as we all do, but I took it as I am to submit to this authority. He needed to deal with his own personal issues rather than put them on me, and because he wouldn't do that, it harmed me instead of protecting me. Therefore, I felt unloved, used, uncared for, like a child to him. This created a trust issue for me, and eventually, I felt as though my marriage will never be any better, so I broke trust by seeking the missing pieces and finding them in other areas rather than placing my heart with Jeff. He proved to be incapable of taking care of it, little lone dealing with me. Then his issue became a trust issue because I had broken his trust. So that needed to be dealt with. Each time I would try to deal with it, repent, self-examine, and cry out to Jesus, then Jeff would be controlling my behaviors and actions a little more aggressively each time. This done the opposite of love and intensified fear, magnified rebellion, and brought on bitterness. So then not only did I feel tremendous fear towards him, but I built walls, I was beginning to be bitter towards him, and felt very stuck in an abusive relationship called marriage. He in return, carried unforgiveness, resentfulness, and a compression of 40 years of emotions and feelings he had yet to release. Jeff and I were quite the hot mess express.

- **Do I have to love and forgive them?**

Your abuser will never think they have done anything wrong. They will most likely never apologize and you won't get the outcome you desire. Once you realize you're being abused, you will want your abuser to know what they are doing. If you can just explain they will understand and stop what they are doing. This won't happen. I'm sorry. Unless they allow God to do a work in them, they will never change.

- **Can I still love someone and set boundaries with them? How do I set boundaries?**

Respect

Acknowledgment

Dignity

Esteem

Appreciation

Warmth

Empathy

Shared sentiments

Kind words

Accurate information

Open communication

Attentiveness

Care

Equality

- **How do I know when and address when a boundary I set is crossed?**

- **How do I know when to cut ties with someone toxic?**

If you are in an unhealthy or abusive relationship, you have a choice to make. If you have been living unaware and have concluded after reading this information that you are in a bad relationship it is now your responsibility to decide what is healthy and safe for you. No one else can make this decision. No one else may know you are a victim. Setting healthy boundaries stepping away from the relationship, or even ending it might be necessary. You should never stay in an unsafe or toxic relationship.

- **What is an addiction?**

(My personal definition) – Something; is anything, that is setting your brain off to crave something, this can be doing something, experiencing a thrill, or a substance. You have the draw to it again and again because it releases chemicals that are enjoyable or feel good, but only for a short time creating a strong hold on you. I believe lust is a form of addiction, as it is a very strong desire, just as impure thoughts. Evil acts fall under sexual immorality and become a craving if not stopped. Once an addiction is formed, I believe you cannot fully stop it without the help of God. Our willpower is not enough, we must ask Him to free us. If you are a believer and seeking Jesus you will know when you fall victim to sinful behavior, it is your choice whether you choose to acknowledge or ignore it.

1. Can Christians live in adultery or with an addiction? While I was studying for the content, I wanted to include in this section I found there were thousands of google searches for this question or a form of it. If I am divorced, if I am living with someone, will I still go to heaven? We can have assurance in salvation by believing Christ died for our sins and asking Him into our hearts and lives. Jesus said in John 3:5, that unless a man be born again, he cannot see the kingdom of God. Now, this is not a free pass to sin. If you feel you are doing something wrong, living wrong, acting, or behaving wrong, and you are a believer, you should have a desire inside of you to turn away from what it is you are doing. The battle of the flesh will always be a battle of the mind as well. In James 4:17 we are told if we know to do good and do it not, to us it is sin. Jesus loves you enough to come after you again and again. Ask yourself these questions:

   1. If Jesus visited me today, would I be embarrassed?
   2. If Jesus came back today, am I ready?
   3. Do I feel overall peace in all areas of my life?

In closing...

Now I said all that to say this. If you are in any type of situation that requires some attention or have felt for a while you are suffering, use the resources I have shared to evaluate and self-examine. This is not for you to construct or invent something that is not real or not there. Perhaps someone is going through a lot or has other issues and some of their behaviors are coming across as inconsiderate or ugly, don't take this information and make a mountain out of a molehill. If you do not have abuse in your life, YOU DO NOT WANT IT.

In all things, pray. Take all issues and self-examination to God. As another person can not tell you what to do, but He can. He can and will always point you in the right direction.

I wrote this series because God laid it on my heart to do so. I have noticed a serious issue within the church, where we are not encouraged to talk about our struggles, pains, fears, and any sort of abuse or abusive situations. Often it is quite opposite, to submit to, endure it, turn the other cheek, and love them to Jesus. It was difficult for me to write this in ways as it is not easy to call out nor is it popular. There is most certainly a fine line between abuse and character qualities. A fine line between needing to simply set some boundaries or leaving. It is difficult for me to share with the church to be guarded of this type of behavior as divorce and "getting even" or "being aggressive" is not God's best. While I have not always acted, reacted, and handled all my situations, and abusive relationships correctly I do know. I must keep marching on. Nobody is going to get it right, no parent, no boss, no Christian, no person ever.

God not only gave me permission to stop my abusive situations but instructed me to do so, then to share it with others. Because I know God has my back, that is easy, because it is a sensitive subject, that is hard. So, if you read this and didn't understand it, it's probably not for you. If you read this and are confused by some things you have been involved in, perhaps you should read on. If you read this and need help, continue reading and check out the resources below, and most of all know, that you are not alone. God loves you and there are people who want you to talk to them, not just end your life or compress the pain. Life can be hard, which is why we need Jesus and each other. Reach out and get help. You are cherished, chosen, and highly favored.

Love Becky

Resources...

Remember you are not alone, God is for you, establish and grow a relationship with Him first and foremost. Then find a great support group like a church, small group, or healthy friends who support and encourage you. If you need to, check yourself into a safe place, or seek therapy, counseling, coaching, or need immediate help, here are some resources:

The following are available 24 hours, 7 days a week

911 for immediate danger or emergency

National domestic violence hotline 1-800-799-7233

www.thehotline.org

National Human Trafficking Hotline 1-888-373-7888

If you are seeking out help for a child, check out these organizations:

Bikers Against Child Abuse® International | Breaking The Chains Of Abuse (bacaworld.org) 1-866-71-ABUSE

Missouri Baptist Children's Home (mbch.org)

As you can probably tell by now, I speak to those who are in or just coming out of a place of trauma, crisis, or pain. I want to include a great book by Dr. Alexander Chapman, The Dialectical Behavior Therapy Skills Workbook for anger, there are others in this series by Dr. Chatman. This will help you to identify with being the abuser, if that is you and you find yourself wanting change and growth to be a part of your life. You are already off to a great start as I have just shared some helpful insight with you from the other side.

Dr. Henry Cloud has helped me greatly in my walk of seeking out God's truth regarding boundaries and abuse. If you really want to dissect the topic, read his book Boundaries! I believe every person in the world should read this!

With her permission I invite you to connect with my personal coach and friend, Bri Peterson. Bri is an abuse coach You can find her on TikTok @abuse_is_abuse or here to book a session www.bpwelnesscoaching.com

Find additional resources in the back of my other books, and on my website. Visit my website for a free safety plan

Practice good self-care. Find more at www.growwithbecky.com

- Have you eaten today?

- Have you had a glass of water?

- Have you showered or brushed your teeth today?

- Write yourself a kind note! Because you are enough, highly favored, and greatly loved.

Becky does signature breakout sessions customized to your group's specific needs around growth. This is an example of a custom short study created for a breakout session for the Women of Audacious Faith, Audacious Faith Conference 2021. Can the rush grow up without mire? Can the flag grow without water? Guide Your growth was the name of this session. Your company has rights to each custom study guide, all of Becky's study guides are created to use multiple times throughout the year. Quarterly is idea for brining your group, team, or class together to do a refresh on the guide from the conference. Becky is also available to do a quarterly group coaching both in person and virtual for company growth and production.

Customizable topics for your company's break out session, with the Bex M Zone's or discover and customize your own:

- The Growth Zone

  Understanding personal space and having a why
  How to create a personal growth plan
  Taking small steps to achieve big goals and dreams

- The Overcomers Zone

  Overcoming toxic behaviors both in yourself and others
  Knowing when to say no and how
  Learning your identity and your truth

- Standing Alone Zone

  Dealing with Fear, shame, and struggles
  Creating a vision board
  Letting go of people pleasing & posture 101

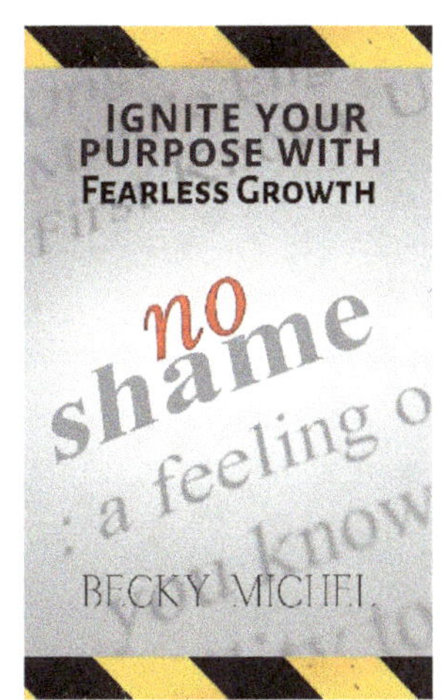

IGNITE YOUR PURPOSE WITH Fearless Growth
no shame
BECKY MICHEL

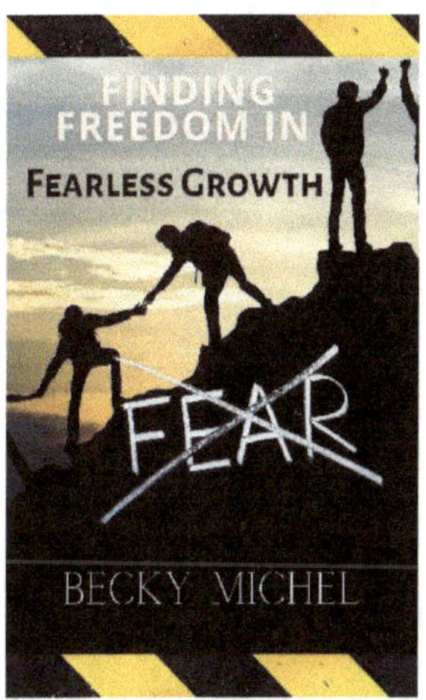

FINDING FREEDOM IN
Fearless Growth
FEAR
BECKY MICHEL

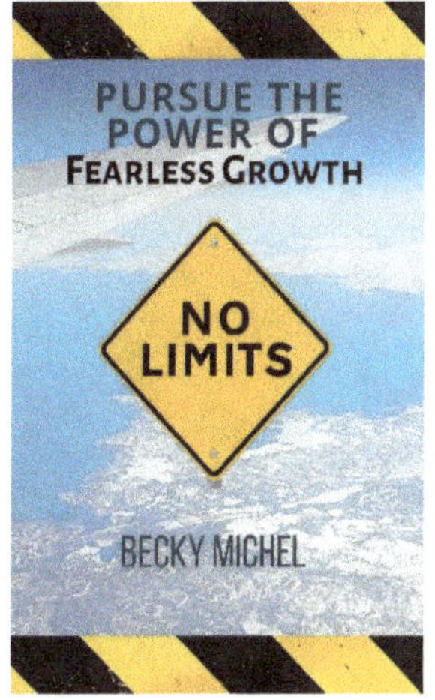

PURSUE THE POWER OF
Fearless Growth
NO LIMITS
BECKY MICHEL

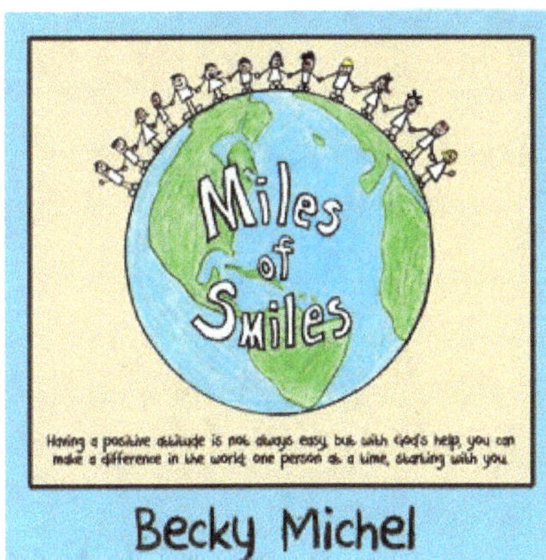

Miles of Smiles
Having a positive attitude is not always easy, but with God's help, you can make a difference in the world one person at a time, starting with you.
Becky Michel

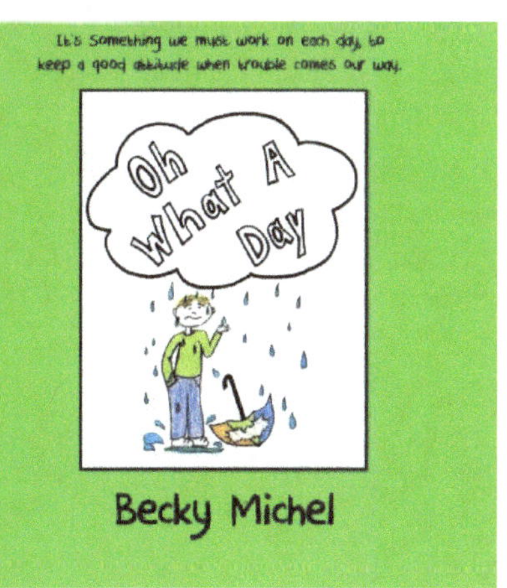

It's something we must work on each day, to keep a good attitude when trouble comes our way.
Oh What A Day
Becky Michel